BOXING

Clive Gifford

WAYLAND

Printed in 2012

Wayland
338 Euston Road
London NW1 3BH

Wayland Australia
Level 17/207 Kent Street
Sydney NSW 2000

Commissioning Editor: Jennifer Sanderson
Designer: Robert Walster, Big Blue Design
Illustrator: Ian Thompson
Picture Researcher: Clive Gifford

Picture Acknowledgements:
The author and publisher would like to thank the following agencies for allowing these
pictures to be reproduced: VANDERLEI ALMEIDA/AFP/Getty: 3, 25; Photo by Jarrett Baker/Getty Images:
19; Al Bello/Allsport/Getty Images: 41; Al Bello/Getty Images: 7, 35; Photo by Andrew D. Bernstein/Getty
Images: 23; GABRIEL BOUYS/AFP/Getty Images: 32; TIMOTHY A. CLARY/AFP/Getty Images: 16;
JACQUES DEMARTHON/AFP/Getty Images: 13; Photo by James Drake/Sports Illustrated/Getty Images:
33; Photo by Elsa/Getty Images: 17; DON EMMERT/AFP/Getty Images: 38; MIKE FIALA/AFP/Getty Images:
12; Jami Garrison/iStockphoto: 44; John Gichigi/Allsport/Getty Images: 5, 22; Photo by John Gichigi/Getty
Images: 15, 18, 36, 37, 39; Photo by John Iacono/Sports Illustrated/Getty Images: 14; JOE
KLAMAR/AFP/Getty Images: 6; JENS-ULRICH KOCH/AFP/Getty Images: 11; Photo by Nick Laham/Getty
Images: 29; Photo by Michael J. LeBrecht II/Sports Illustrated/Getty Images: 31; DAMIEN
MEYER/AFP/Getty Images: 20; Photo by Ethan Miller/Getty Images: COVER, 21, 27, 40; KAZUHIRO
NOGI/AFP/Getty Images: 30; Photo by Hy Peskin/Time Life Pictures/Getty Images: 43; MIGUEL
ROJO/AFP/Getty Images: 28; Photo by Martin Rose/Bongarts/Getty Images: 8; CARL DE SOUZA/AFP/Getty
Images: 26; STAFF/AFP/Getty Images: 9; Holly Stein/Allsport/Getty Images: 24; Holly Stein/Getty Images:
42; OMAR TORRES/AFP/Getty Images: 34

British Library Cataloguing in Publication Data
  Gifford, Clive
  Boxing. - (Inside sport)
  1. Boxing - Juvenile literature
  I. Title II. Series
  796.8'3-dc22

ISBN: 978 0 7502 6952 0

Printed in China

Wayland is a division of Hachette Children's Books,
an Hachette UK company
www.hachette.co.uk

First published in 2010 by Wayland

This paperback edition published in 2012 by Wayland

CONTENTS

INTRODUCTION

Boxing is an individual combat sport requiring power, speed, skill and courage. It has captivated millions of fans all over the world with its intense demands and challenges.

Boxing's Appeal

Millions of fans are hooked on boxing because of the skill and bravery displayed by boxers and the thrill of two opponents standing toe to toe to prove which one of them is the best. Over the years, the sport has been graced by some magnificent champions, such as Sugar Ray Robinson, Joe Louis and the most famous boxer of them all, Muhammad Ali. Greats in recent times include Floyd Mayweather Jr, Joe Calzaghe and Oscar de la Hoya.

Kazakhstan's Bakhyt Sarsekbayev (left) in action during the 2008 Olympic Games, where he won a gold medal. Amateur boxers, such as those taking part in the Olympics, wear vests and headgear that are prohibited in professional boxing.

Manny Pacquiao (right) strikes Ricky Hatton with an uppercut to the chin during their 2009 IBO World Championship fight in Las Vegas. Pacquaio won the fight in the second round.

Amateur and Professional

Thousands of men and women learn to box to build fitness. Some never enter a ring, but just work on the moves using padded bags and punch balls as targets. Others seek out the challenge of fighting against an opponent in sparring (practice sessions) or in competitive bouts. Amateur boxing is thriving worldwide in over 180 countries, with local, regional and national tournaments as well as headline competitions such as the Olympics and World Championships. Some amateurs turn professional where they are paid to compete in fights.

Rounds and Breaks

In the distant past, bouts could last for several hours. Today, strict rules govern the length of a fight. Boxing action is split into timed rounds, usually with a one minute break between each round. In amateur boxing, bouts normally last four rounds, each being two minutes long. In 2009, this was altered for male adult amateurs to three rounds of three minutes each. The action is frenetic and boxers can be exhausted by the final round. Some professional fights are fought over four or six rounds. Up until the 1980s, professional championship bouts tended to be over 15 rounds, but today they are held over 12 three-minute-long rounds.

MAD FACT

In 1893, Jack Burke fought Andrew Bowen in New Orleans for a total of 110 rounds. The bout ended in a draw!

Boxing was popular in ancient Egypt and Sumeria (southern Iraq) more than 4,000 years ago. In 688BCE it featured at the ancient Greek Olympic games with competitors wearing thongs around their wrists for protection. The ancient Romans added metal spikes to the thongs, resulting in fights to the death.

London Revival

Boxing began to become popular in London from the 17th century onwards. In 1719, James Figg opened a boxing school there, teaching self-defence and challenging all-comers to take him on. One of Figg's pupils, James Broughton, was crowned British champion in 1729 and drew up one of the first sets of rules. Bare-knuckle boxing boomed in popularity in Britain and in the United States during the 19th century, with Bristol's Tom Cribb one of the sport's first superstars. It is said that his fights attracted as many as 30,000 spectators. In 1869, John Sholto Douglas, the 8th Marquess of Queensberry, drew up a new set of rules that were adopted all over the world. Boxers were required to wear padded gloves, wrestling and holding were not allowed and rounds lasted three minutes.

MAD FACT

In Roman times, slaves were forced to fight each other in a circle marked on the ground. This is where the term 'boxing ring' comes from.

Cecilia Braekhus (right) and Vinni Skovgaard square up to each during their 2009 world championship fight. Braekhus, a former champion kickboxer from Norway, won the bout.

Who is...

...Sugar Ray Robinson?

Sugar Ray Robinson (real name Walker Smith Jr) was one of the world's greatest ever boxers. Born in 1921, he had an amazing career as an amateur boxer, during which he won all of his 80-plus fights, 69 of which were knockouts. Turning professional at the age of 19, he fought without losing for 40 fights before he was beaten by Jake La Motta. Robinson recovered to win six world titles, five at middleweight and one at welterweight. In total he fought an amazing 201 professional bouts. Flamboyant in and out of the ring and travelling with his own entourage of supporters, Robinson was immensely popular and became the prototype of many modern top professional boxers.

Sugar Ray Robinson (right) fights Jake La Motta in an epic bout in 1951. Considered one of the greatest bouts of all time, this was the pair's sixth encounter.

Modern Developments

While many of the key rules altered little, weight divisions (see p20) and many different championships were developed in the last century. Today, greater emphasis is placed on boxers' health and safety. Despite being a demonstration sport at the 1904 Olympics, women's boxing was outlawed in most countries until the late 1980s. The first professional fight to be sanctioned by the Boxing Board of Control in Britain was between Jane Couch and Simona Lukic in 1998. In 2001 the first amateur women's European Championships and the first World Championships took place.

MAD FACT

In one of the first women's boxing matches in the United States in 1876 the prize was a silver butter dish.

AIM OF THE SPORT

Boxers fight, striking their opponent using only their hands, which are covered in protective gloves. Boxers aim to win a fight by knocking their opponent out, forcing them to retire or to win the fight on points according to the opinion of the judges, which is known as winning by a decision.

Knockout!

The most spectacular end to a fight is when a boxer is knocked out (KO'd). A KO occurs when the boxer hits the floor after a legal punch or series of punches and cannot regain his feet and recover within a referee's count of ten seconds. If a fighter is hit to the floor but recovers inside the referee's count, it is a knockdown and, providing the referee decides that the boxer is fit to continue, the bout carries on. In some forms of boxing, three knockdowns in the same round count the same as a knockout and the fight is ended.

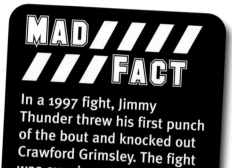

MAD FACT

In a 1997 fight, Jimmy Thunder threw his first punch of the bout and knocked out Crawford Grimsley. The fight was over in 13 seconds!

Technical Knockout

A referee can stop a fight at any time if it is felt that one boxer is taking too many punches, is not in a position to defend himself well or has suffered a bad injury, such as a closed eye or broken jaw or nose. A fight doctor can examine a boxer and decide if the fight should be stopped. A boxer's corner can also end a fight by throwing in the towel or stepping into the ring. When a fight ends in any of these ways, it is known as a TKO – a technical knockout. If a boxer decides to quit, it also counts as a technical knockout.

STAT ATTACK

KO Percentage
The number of wins a boxer completes via knocking out their opponent is their career KO percentage. Here are the KO percentages of some of the world's leading boxers.

Vitali Klitschko	won 43	KO 88.89%
Miguel Cotto	won 37	KO 76.92%
Joe Calzaghe	won 46	KO 69.57%
Oscar de la Hoya	won 39	KO 66.67%
Manny Pacquaio	won 54	KO 64.41%
Floyd Mayweather Jr	won 42	KO 61.9%
Bernard Hopkins	won 52	KO 52.46%

Going the Distance

When a fight goes the distance (lasts the scheduled maximum number of rounds), the role of the fight judges becomes crucial. In some smaller bouts, the referee decides the winner, lifting the arm of the victorious boxer. In most professional boxing the fight is scored by three judges who sit ringside. They score each round based on the quantity and quality of punches, as well as which boxer shows the most aggression, defence and skill. A knockdown loses the fallen fighter a point. The referee can also deduct points from a boxer for a foul (see p17).

(see p17)

MAD //// //// FACT

In Ken Norton's 31st professional fight, he beat Muhammad Ali. For his previous fight, against Charlie Reno, Norton had been paid just US$300.

Amateur Scoring

In amateur boxing, winning on points is the main aim of a bout. A point is scored when a punch connects firmly with a scoring area – the central part of the torso and the head. The punch must have the weight of the boxer's shoulder or body behind it for it to score. The punch must be made using the knuckle area of the glove. Most amateur boxing gloves have a white scoring area on them to aid the judges. The referee can stop a fight for these reasons:

- opponent outclassed (RSCO)
- opponent outscored (RSCOS)
- injury to either boxer (RSCI)
- head injury (RSCH).

Giant Russian heavyweight Nicolai Valuev (right) walks to the neutral corner after knocking down American Clifford Etienne in their 2005 heavyweight bout. Etienne failed to make the count, giving victory to Valuev in the third round.

EQUIPMENT AND SAFETY

Boxing is an impact sport so carries with it some risk of injury. In amateur boxing, that risk is greatly reduced by the wearing of padded protective headgear, shorter fights and strict safety rules.

Hands and Gloves

A boxer's safety equipment starts with the boxing gloves that he uses to hit his opponent. These are padded to protect the hands from the impact of a punch. By adding weight to the boxer's hand, they also slightly decrease the speed and force of the impact on the opponent. Underneath their gloves, boxers can use up to 5.48m of bandage-like material, called hand wraps. These are wrapped carefully around the hand and wrist to help protect some of the smaller hand bones. In major fights, a member of the opponent's corner is allowed to watch the wraps being placed on a boxer.

Julio César Chávez (left) trains with a sparring partner. Both boxers are wearing full protective gear, which includes padded sparring helmets and gloves.

Protective Equipment

A gumshield is always worn during bouts and also when sparring. It protects teeth from being knocked out following a blow to the mouth. For male boxers, a groin protector is slipped into an inside front pouch in their shorts to protect against a painful low blow – a punch well below the belt of their shorts. When sparring, boxers also wear protective headgear and padding.

Medical Matters

Boxers can suffer injuries, such as torn or strained muscles, blisters on feet from roadwork (see p18) or broken bones. The most serious potential injuries come in fights where repeated impact from punches to the head can cause concussion or, at its most severe, brain damage and even death. Since the death in the 1980s of Korean boxer Duk Koo Kim, all amateur boxers have to gain a medical certificate before they are allowed to take part in bouts. In Britain, professional boxers have to have an MRI scan and other health checks every year. If they are knocked out in a bout, they cannot fight again for at least 45 days.

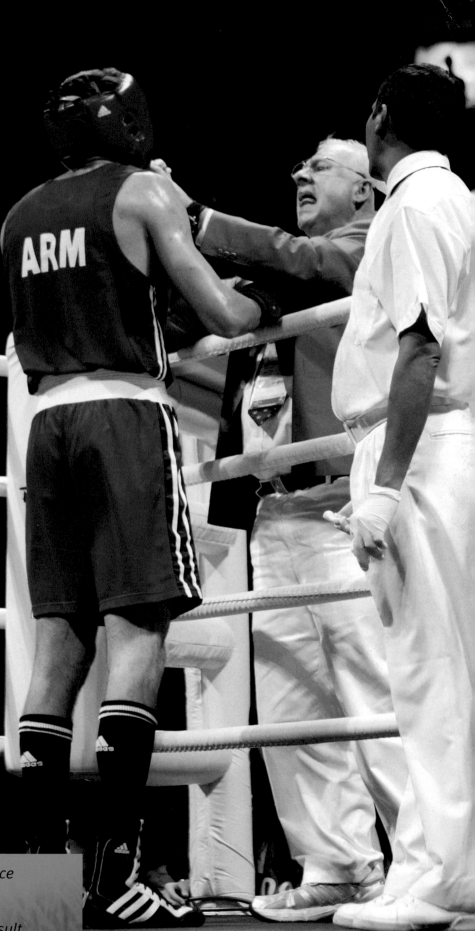

A fight doctor checks the cuts on the face of Armenian boxer Andranik Hakobyan during the 2008 Olympics. The doctor ordered the bout to be stopped as a result.

IN THE RING

Boxing action takes place inside a square arena called a ring. This is raised up off the floor and surrounded by a series of ropes that are fastened to 1.5m-tall padded support posts in the four corners.

Ring Dimensions

Boxing rings vary in size according to the organisation running the particular fight. In international amateur boxing governed by the AIBA, for example, the ring is between 4.9 and 6.1 metres square. If the ring is to be used in AIBA international championships, it has to be 6.1m in size. Some professional boxing organisations allow a large ring size, up to 7.315m in the case of the WBC. The floor of the ring usually has around 2.5cm of padding covered in tough canvas. Resin powder is sometimes sprinkled over the canvas to provide grip. If this is the case, referees often wipe the gloves of any boxer who has been knocked down or slipped and touched the floor with his gloves as the resin could cause eye damage.

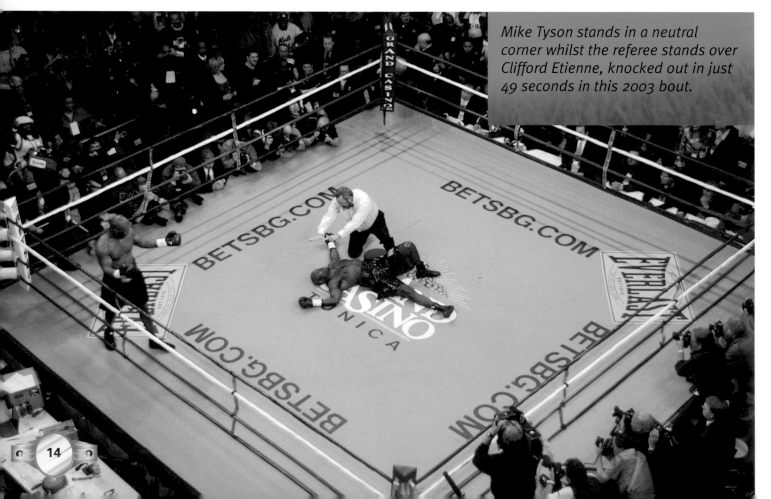

Mike Tyson stands in a neutral corner whilst the referee stands over Clifford Etienne, knocked out in just 49 seconds in this 2003 bout.

On the Ropes

In the past, the ropes surrounding the ring were sometimes very loose and elastic, allowing boxers to lean back great distances, often dangerously. Today, they are taut but will give when a boxer leans his bodyweight onto them. On the very rare occasion that boxers do fall through the ropes and out of the ring, they have 20 seconds to return to the ring. If this does not happen, they are considered knocked out and the fight is ended.

MAD /// /// FACT

Jerry Boyd worked as a cuts-man for decades but he was also a writer. Two of his stories were turned into the film *Million Dollar Baby*.

Mexican boxer Jose Luis Castillo sits in his corner as his trainer (left) issues instructions and his cuts-man works on his forehead. Castillo narrowly won this 2007 fight against Herman Ngoudjo of Cameroon.

A Boxer's Corner

One corner of the ring is reserved for each boxer with the other two known as neutral corners. A referee may direct one boxer to stand in a neutral corner while he checks on the condition of the other boxer or gives him a warning for a rule infringement. The boxer's trainer (or coach for an amateur boxer) will be in his corner. He is the main person in charge of conditioning the boxer and deciding on fight strategy. In addition, there are an assistant trainer, who may give the boxer water and a towel, and a cuts-man, who repairs damage to his boxer's face. The role of the cuts-man can be crucial, especially in long, bruising fights. Many bouts are stopped by the referee due to heavy bleeding on a boxer's face or swelling that may cause an eye to close.

THE REFEREE AND RULES

A referee runs every bout. He ensures that the rules are followed, helps guarantee the safety of the two boxers and does his best to allow a good, fair fight to take place.

The Man in Charge

A referee is in charge of both boxers and their corners' conduct. He can warn corner men who enter the ring early or leave it late and can warn boxers, deduct points from their score or disqualify them for breaking the rules. A boxer cannot hold, trip, kick or push an opponent nor hit him with a shoulder, forearm or elbow. If boxers are holding each other, a referee will order the boxers to 'break'. Boxers have to take a full step back and must not try to punch during the process – this is a rule infringement called hitting on the break.

Clean and Dirty Punches

A boxer is allowed to hit the head and upper body of his opponent but not the back of the head or the lower body. All strikes have to be above the belt, otherwise a low blow is signalled. A boxer hit with an accidental low blow has up to five minutes to recover. If he cannot, he is considered knocked out. A boxer making a low blow or other form of rule-breaking punch usually receives a warning from the referee. If it occcurs again, points are deducted.

Referee Arthur Mercante Jr steps in to break up Carlos Baldomir and Zab Judah during their championship fight for three titles in 2006. Mercante's father, Arthur Sr, refereed over 140 championship bouts.

Disqualifications

A referee can disqualify a fighter if he is guilty of repeated fouls or particularly serious fouls such as kicking a knocked down opponent. If a foul causes an injury but the bout continues, the referee orders the judges to deduct two points from the boxer who caused the injury. If the foul results in an injury that means the fight ends immediately, the boxer who committed the foul is disqualified. The most famous disqualification occurred in 1997 when Mike Tyson bit off part of Evander Holyfield's ear.

A referee, wearing white rubber gloves in case he comes into contact with blood, issues a count to Brandon Jackson after he has been knocked down by fellow American boxer Josiah Judah.

Accidents and No Decisions

A referee can end a fight early if he fears for one boxer's health or inability to defend himself. He can also signal the end of the bout if an accident or serious foul play occurs. In fights where an accident leaves one fighter unable to continue, the judges add up their points to determine the winner. If fewer than four rounds have occurred, the bout is usually declared a no decision and usually a re-match is organised. This happened to Robert Guerrero and Daud Yordan in 2009, when an accidental clash of heads led to the fight being stopped in the second round due to bleeding.

IN TRAINING

Although they train exceptionally hard before a fight, boxers must carry their maximum intensity into the ring. This is where the trainer and a good training programme come into their own, as the boxer's exercise workload is carefully reduced before the fight.

Power and Stamina

Boxers need great power in their arms and shoulders to land telling punches. They also need stamina to be able to make punches again and again. In a 2007 fight against Mikkel Kessler, for example, Joe Calzaghe threw more than 1,000 punches during the 12 rounds. Boxers also require great strength in their legs and incredible fitness to keep on moving throughout a fight. A boxer's training will include lots of roadwork, running great distances outside or on a treadmill, as well as interval training, working hard for a short period and then taking a shorter rest before repeating the exercise.

Skills Training

Boxers work on their skills throughout their training. They use speed balls for quick, repetitive punching to build their hand speed and heavy punch bags to work on power hitting. Sometimes, different punches and movements are worked with the boxer's trainer wearing padded focus mitts that they position as targets for the boxer to hit. A

US boxer Paulie Malignaggi trains with a speed ball four days before his 2008 world title fight against Britain's Ricky Hatton. Boxers move around the speed ball to attack from different angles.

...Joe Calzaghe?

Welsh boxer Joe Calzaghe retired in 2009 after a glorious career during which he was always trained by his father, Enzo. He won four schoolboy ABA titles before turning professional in 1993 and became a feared, difficult opponent, famed for his skill and fitness. During this career, he claimed the scalps of Chris Eubank, Richie Woodhall and Jeff Lacy amongst others. Calzaghe held the WBO super middleweight title from 1997 to 2008 – the longest reign of any recent champion at any weight. He relinquished the title only to move up to light-heavyweight to challenge and beat Bernard Hopkins. He followed this with a victory over boxing legend Roy Jones Jr to retire as world champion with a perfect record – 46 wins from 46 fights.

Joe Calzaghe (right) works on his punch combinations, aiming for focus pads worn by his father and trainer, Enzo.

boxer will also work on his flexibility, so that he can lean, duck, bob and weave to avoid his opponent's punches.

Sparring

Sparring is usually carried out inside a boxing ring as a boxer moves, punches and defends against a prepared opponent. Boxers wear headgear and groin protectors while sparring. Usually they and their sparring partner use heavier, more padded gloves that cause less painful impact. The sparring partner will be briefed beforehand by the boxer's trainer to work on a specific aspect, such as close defence or attack using a specific combination of punches.

MAD ///// ///// FACT

Joe Calzaghe was 17 years old when he was defeated by Romanian Adrian Opreda in a bout at the 1990 European Junior Championships. That was the last fight he lost!

MAKING THE WEIGHT

Boxing pits fighters of roughly the same size against each other by grading boxers according to their weight.

Light to Heavy

Boxing was initially open to all-comers, giving big, heavy men huge advantages over much smaller and lighter opponents. These advantages were not just weight but also reach and height. Reach is the effective length of a boxer's arms. A boxer with a greater reach than his opponent is able to punch from longer distances.

In the early 20th century, eight weight divisions were established, from flyweight to heavyweight. Today, many amateur competitions feature 11 divisions, while professional boxing features 17 or more, from light flyweight for fighters weighing up to 49kg to heavyweight for boxers weighing more than 88.5kg.

At the Weigh-In

A boxer's weight is measured at the weigh-in shortly before a fight. Officials check that boxers are below the maximum weight for their division. If they are not, boxers are given a

In professional boxing, there is no upper limit for the heavyweight division. At the weigh-in for their 2008 bout, Nikolai Valuev (right) weighed-in at 141kg, 43.8kg more than his opponent, Evander Holyfield.

window, usually two or three hours, to try to lose weight via a workout, sauna or some other method. If they still fail to make the weight, then if the fight is a professional bout for a title it is usually cancelled or rescheduled as a non-title bout. At major amateur events with multiple bouts, such as the Olympics, boxers have to make the weight every day that they box. At the 2008 Olympics, world amateur boxing champion, Britain's gold-medal hope Frankie Gavin failed to make the 60kg limit for the lightweight division and was forced to withdraw.

MAD //// //// FACT

Frenchman Georges Carpentier began his professional career as a flyweight at the age of 14. He went on to win bouts in every weight division, including heavyweight.

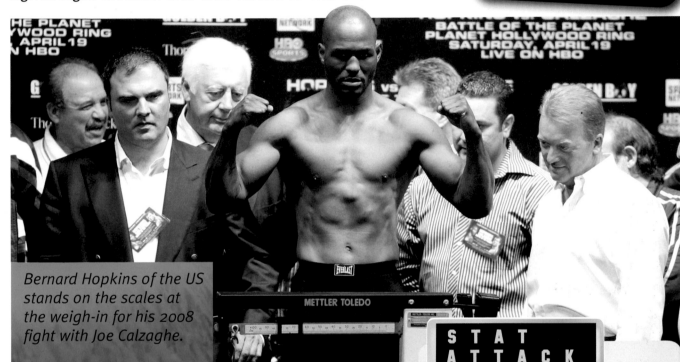

Bernard Hopkins of the US stands on the scales at the weigh-in for his 2008 fight with Joe Calzaghe.

Moving up the Weights

Most boxers fight in a single weight division for much or all of their careers. Some, however, move up the weights, taking on bigger opponents. With only three kilograms between each lower weight division, many boxers can easily bulk up to gain the extra weight. However, they may lack the height, reach and possible power advantage of naturally bigger fighters. US boxer Thomas Hearns is regarded as a boxing legend as he won world titles at six different weights: welterweight, super welter, middle, super middle, light heavy and cruiserweight.

STAT ATTACK

Weight Divisions at the Olympics

Division	Weight Limit
Light flyweight	49 kg
Flyweight	51 kg
Bantamweight	54 kg
Featherweight	57 kg
Lightweight	61 kg
Light welterweight	64 kg
Welterweight	67 kg
Middleweight	73 kg
Light heavyweight	80 kg
Heavyweight	91 kg
Super heavyweight	No limit

STANCE AND MOVEMENT

A boxer's basic body position is called his stance. All boxing movements start from this stance, which is why it is practised and refined by boxers at all levels of ability.

Orthodox or Southpaw

Boxers have two basic choices of stance: orthodox or southpaw. In an orthodox stance, the boxer's left foot and left side of his body face forwards. The turning of the body helps reduce the amount of target area of the body that the opponent can easily see and reach. His two feet are roughly hip- or shoulder-width apart with the front knee flexed a little and the rear knee bent a little more. The boxer carries his weight equally on the balls of both feet. The aim of the stance is to provide a steady, firm base with the body balanced and able to move easily in any direction from this point. A southpaw stance bears all these points in mind but is performed the other way round, with the right foot and right side of the body to the front.

MAD FACT

Sugar Ray Leonard intended to go to university but family money worries meant that he decided to become a professional boxer instead.

Renowned southpaw, British boxer Naseem Hamed, leads with a right jab onto the nose of Vuyani Bungu of South Africa during their WBO featherweight championship fight. Hamed fought 37 professional fights, only losing one.

Who is...

...Sugar Ray Leonard?

America's Sugar Ray Leonard was renowned for his lightning-fast footwork and slick, powerful punching. He enjoyed a highly successful amateur career with more than 140 victories, including a gold medal in the 1976 Olympics in the welterweight division. He turned professional in 1977 and won his first world title just two years later. Despite retiring and then taking part in frequent comeback fights during the 1980s, he is remembered as the standout boxer of that decade, winning world championships at five different weights.

Sugar Ray Leonard (right) fights Thomas Hearns in their WBC super middleweight title fight in Las Vegas in 1989. This thrilling bout, during which Leonard was knocked down twice, ended in a draw.

Taking Guard

A crucial part of the stance is the position of the hands, arms and head in relation to the stance. The general starting position is called taking guard. The right hand is usually held beside the chin, with the forearm pointing down along the body. The left hand is held out a few inches in front of the face with the elbow bent. The elbows are tucked in to protect the sides of the body, but the arms remain relaxed, not stiff so that a boxer can tense his muscles and snap out a quick punch. A combination of a good stance and guard gives a boxer the chance to block or dodge punches. It also gives him a firm and solid base from which to throw his own punches.

Footwork and Movement

A boxer's basic footwork consists of short, sliding steps that help keep him balanced. The foot nearest the direction in which the boxer is heading is moved first, with the other foot following it. A boxer's legs should never cross, as if they do, he will lose his balance.

MAD FACT

In 2006, a boxing first occurred at the Muncie Horizon Centre in Indiana, USA when Al Hughes, his son, Al, and his daughter, Angela, all fought bouts at the same event. All three won!

DEFENCE

No boxer can win without a solid and skilful defence. This involves being watchful of the opponent's movements, as well as being able to react quickly to avoid or limit the impact of punches.

Bobbing and Weaving

Many boxers bob and weave to present their opponents with a constantly moving target that is harder to hit. Boxers bounce slightly on the balls of their feet, keeping the head moving while the body twists at the waist. Their elbows cover much of their body from shots while they try not to move back and forth predictably. Bobbing and weaving uses up energy and boxers are likely to employ it less as a long, tiring bout progresses.

Blocks and Parries

Blocks and parries deflect or stop a punch before it can land fully on its target. In most circumstances, punches aimed towards the head are blocked with the glove, while those aimed at the body are blocked with the arm or elbow. A parry is used over longer range, with the boxer pushing his opponent's punching hand to the side.

Italy's Giovanni Parisi sways back to avoid contact with a right hook thrown by formidable Mexican boxer Julio César Chávez.

Brazilian boxer Dean Pereira covers up to protect himself from an attack from Mexico's Carlos Cuadras during their semi-final clash at the 2007 Pan-American Games.

Footwork and Movement

Boxers with experience use the flexibility in their bodies, as well as quick reactions, to bend their back or neck to duck or sway out of the line of some punches. Good boxers try to use the whole of the ring and, at times, employ quick footwork to retreat from a persistent attack. They also sometimes pivot on their feet to turn and change the angles to put off their opponent and to get into a good position to launch an attack of their own.

MAD FACT

Mike Tyson is the youngest man to win a world heavyweight championship. He was just 20 years old when he beat Trevor Berbick in 1986.

Covering Up

Boxers forced into a corner or on the ropes will try to cover up to protect as much of themselves as possible. The most common form of covering up is the full cover, where the hands are held high in front of the cheeks with the chin tucked in and the elbows close to each side. Another technique to buy a short rest from an attack is clinching. This is when a boxer hugs his opponent, effectively trapping his opponent's arms so that he cannot punch.

JABS AND STRAIGHTS

There are a range of punches used in boxing. They are usually divided into the jab and all other types of shots, known as power punches.

David Haye jabs fellow Briton Enzo Maccarinelli, the first of a combination of punches Haye threw to knock down his opponent and win the WBO Cruiserweight title.

The Jab

The jab is the first punch a novice boxer learns. It is a simple but important movement as it is the most common punch used in bouts. The jab is thrown with the leading hand – the left hand for a boxer in an orthodox stance and the right hand if he is a southpaw. It is thrown with a slight turn of the shoulder forward and a rapid straightening of the arm. The hand is turned clockwise just before impact to add more snap to the punch. The other hand is held high to protect against any punches from the opponent. In amateur boxing, the jab is a leading points scoring

Philippino boxer Manny Pacquiao is renowned for his hard punching and devastating jab. Pacquiao became WBC Flyweight world champion at the age of 19. He moved up the weights becoming IBF Junior Bantamweight world champion in 2001 and relinquished that title only when he moved up to featherweight in 2004. In 2008 Pacquiao won three world championship titles at different weight divisions. He ended the year rated by many experts as the best pound-for-pound boxer in the world. Pacquiao has been involved in some of the most exciting fights in recent years against Erik Morales, Marco Antonio Barrera, Oscar de la Hoya and Ricky Hatton, who he knocked out in the second round in 2009.

Manny Pacquiao throws a jab at the head of Oscar de la Hoya in their dramatic, all-action 2008 fight. Over the eight rounds of action, the winner, Pacquiao, threw 252 jabs.

punch. It can also be used to keep an opponent at a distance or unbalanced, and can distract him before another, more powerful, shot is launched. The target for a jab is usually the opponent's chin, but jabs to the body are equally important. Many champions have been renowned for the speed, power and effectiveness of their jabs.

Straight Punches

The punch most commonly used in tandem with the left jab is the right straight. It is usually thrown immediately after a left jab but can be used on its own. Southpaw boxers who have a right jab, use their left hand to throw a similar punch. For a boxer in an orthodox stance, the punch is thrown from their guard position, with the right hand by the head, straight across to connect with the opponent's head. The punch can generate a lot of power.

MAD FACT

In his 2009 fight against Antonio Margarito, Shane Moseley threw an average of 37 jabs every round and around 32 other types of punches per round.

PACKING A PUNCH

The two main power punches other than the straight are the hook and the uppercut. These formidable shots, when mixed with jabs and straights, have the potential to win fights.

The Hook

Hooks are thrown from medium to close range and travel up and out before curving back to strike the opponent. The punch's curving path is often out of an opponent's field of vision, surprising the opponent if thrown well. To throw a good left hook, a boxer twists his body at the waist to the left, shifts his weight onto his right foot and keeps his elbow high as the body turns to the right, bringing his fist around to connect.

A boxer must put his bodyweight into the shot. Many boxers, including Joe Frazier, Evander Holyfield and Miguel Cotto were feared for their powerful hooks.

Chris Namus of Uruguay launches a right hook over the guard of Mexico's Perla Hernandez.

Abner Mares (right) makes a solid connection with a right uppercut to the chin of fellow Mexican, Francisco Soto. Mares, fighting at bantamweight, won the bout by a knockout in the fifth round.

The Uppercut

Mostly thrown with the right hand by a boxer in an orthodox stance, the uppercut travels from below the opponent's line of sight upwards to connect with the chin or jaw. An uppercut's force is generated not just by the arm, but by the feet, which drive powerfully upwards with the boxer's weight over his right hip. The uppercut is used mostly at very close range and can sometimes get underneath an opponent's defences, especially if his gloves are held in a high guard position. Although the uppercut is sometimes a fight-ending shot, it comes with risk, too, because it leaves a boxer unprotected should the opponent punch back at the same time. Fighters such as Mike Tyson, Julio César Chávez and Rocky Marciano all had incredibly powerful uppercuts that they used to either soften up or knock out opponents.

Fighting Close In

When fighting close up to the opponent, a boxer may use a range of punches to strike his opponent, including uppercuts and shots that cuff the side of his opponent's head or strike the body. Another punch used at close distance is a straight punch but thrown with a bent elbow, so that the glove travels horizontally into the opponent's stomach or lower chest.

MAD FACT

Mike Tyson was renowned for his powerful uppercut, but it was an uppercut thrown as a combination of punches by his 1990 opponent, James 'Buster' Douglas, that led to Tyson's first defeat in 38 fights.

COMBINATIONS AND COUNTERPUNCHES

Boxers rarely win fights with a single punch. Most punches are thrown in small series known as combinations. Boxers need to pick the right punch at the right time, most especially when counter-attacking.

Punches in Bunches

Boxers are taught to throw 'punches in bunches'. This takes a lot of practice to ensure that the combinations flow well, exert maximum power and leave the boxer balanced at all times. One of the simplest combinations, two or three jabs made in quick succession, is one of the toughest to master. It relies on expert timing to recover the arm back to its starting position to generate enough power in the snap forward for the next.

Japan's WBC Superbantamweight world champion, Toshiaki Nishioka, launches a counter-attack against Thailand's Napapol Kiatisakchokchai.

Who is...

...Oscar de la Hoya?

At his peak, Oscar de la Hoya was one of most fluid and best boxers of his era, often raining down five, six and seven punch combinations with grace and power. He notched up a staggering 223 wins as an amateur and won a gold medal at the 1992 Olympics before turning professional. De la Hoya shied away from no one during his career, during which time he beat an astounding 17 world champions, from Julio César Chávez and Hector Camacho to Arturo Gatti and Pernell Whitaker. He won ten world titles and was enormously popular with fight fans. His bouts have generated more revenue than any other boxer in history and he is now a promoter in charge of Golden Boy Promotions.

Oscar de la Hoya works hard in training. As an amateur he had only six losses in more than 220 bouts and won the United States' only boxing gold medal at the 1992 Olympics.

Common Combinations

The most commonly used combination is the one-two – a left jab followed by a straight right punch for an orthodox boxer, or a right jab followed by a straight left for a southpaw boxer. A good jab will often lift up the opponent's head, allowing a powerful straight right punch to connect with the chin. A left hook can be added to the combination, too. This jab-straight-hook combination is one of the most natural to boxers and, if performed well, can be devastating. Boxers can also switch the focus of their attack by aiming a punch for the head and if the opponent leaves their body unguarded, throw further punches to the body. A strong left jab to the head, for example, can be followed up by a hook to the body.

STAT ATTACK

Most Punches Landed in a Championship Fight

Fighter	Punches Landed	Opponent
Troy Dorsey	620	Jorge Paez
Philip Holiday	555	Ivan Robinson
John Molina	550	Manuel Medina
Pernell Whitaker	526	Santos Cardona
Daniel Zaragoza	504	Wayne McCullough

FIGHTING STYLES

A boxer's physique and his own strengths and weaknesses influence his style of fighting and this, along with a look at his opponent's past fights, will determine his tactics.

MAD //// //// FACT

Despite fighting some of the world's greatest heavyweight punchers in his 61-fight career, Muhammad Ali was never knocked out and retired only once.

In- and Out-Fighters

Many short, stocky boxers prefer to box at close range, or inside, using hooks and uppercuts and a high work-rate to unsettle their opponents. In-fighters look to get in close, especially if their opponent has a longer reach than them. A taller boxer with a longer reach than his opponent may choose to box from a greater distance, scoring well with jabs. Out-fighters need expert footwork as well as very fast hands to make a punch or combination and then move clear of danger. Great out-fighters include Roy Jones Jr, Floyd Mayweather Jr and legends of the past such as Sugar Ray Leonard.

Pressure Fighters and Brawlers

Some boxers press forward, even if they are hit, to throw combinations. These boxers are known as swarmers or pressure fighters. Brawlers are boxing's most aggressive punchers, relying far less on mobility and skill, and often planting their feet on the floor rather than staying on their toes. This means that can put maximum leverage and bodyweight into their shots. Brawlers may have a predictable fighting style with lots of single big punches, but if one or two connect, their opponent could be knocked down.

The 2007 Ricky Hatton v Floyd Mayweather Jr superfight was a clash of fighting styles. Hatton, a renowned pressure fighter, was unable to beat Mayweather's outfighting style.

Who is...

...Muhammad Ali?

Boxing legend Muhammad Ali began boxing as a talented amateur, Cassius Clay, who won an Olympic gold medal in 1960. As a professional, Clay predicted the round in which he would knock out the great Archie Moore and then beat Sonny Liston to win the World Heavyweight title in 1964, the same year he changed his name. He defended his title successfully nine times in the following two years, but was banned for more than three years because he refused to join the army. Ali returned in 1970 to take part in some of the most enthralling contests of that decade, including superfights against Ken Norton, George Foreman and Joe Frazier. In 1978, aged 36, he became world heavyweight champion for the third time, before retiring in 1981.

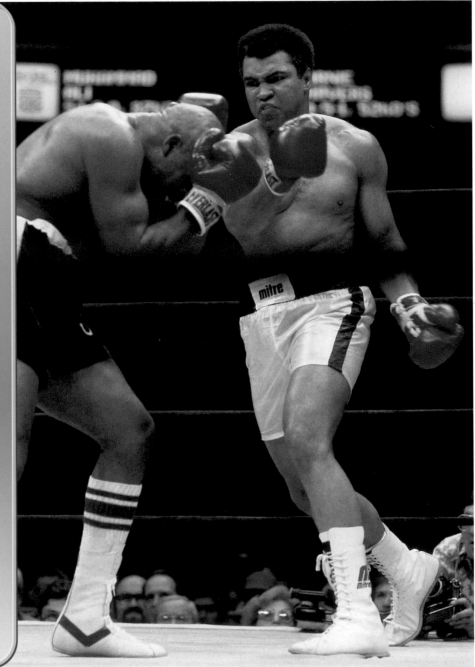

Changing Tactics

While a boxer may prefer a certain fight style, he may be forced to adopt other styles during a bout. If an out-fighter is behind on points, for example, he may choose to come inside and fight as a brawler or in-fighter. Similarly, a brawler may be skilled enough to keep his opponent at distance when ahead and with only a handful of rounds to go.

It is easy to forget that Ali was a big man in the ring, weighing just short of 100kg. This was in part due to his incredible hand speed, his quick, graceful footwork and movement and his keen boxing brain.

AMATEUR BOXING

Amateur competitions usually see a boxer fight a number of opponents on the way to competing for a championship title in a final bout.

Competitions

Boxing appears at a number of multi-sport competitions, including the Commonwealth Games, Pan-American Games and Asian Games. There are a number of important boxing-only international tournaments, too. The European Amateur Boxing Championships were first held in 1925 and are now hosted every two years. In recent times, boxers from Russia and Eastern Europe have dominated the competition. The biggest amateur competition is the World Amateur Championships. These are now held every two years.

The Olympics

Boxing first appeared at the 1904 Olympics. The Games are considered to be one of the pinnacles of amateur boxing. Countries can send a maximum of one boxer per division to the tournament, where

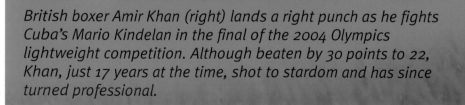

British boxer Amir Khan (right) lands a right punch as he fights Cuba's Mario Kindelan in the final of the 2004 Olympics lightweight competition. Although beaten by 30 points to 22, Khan, just 17 years at the time, shot to stardom and has since turned professional.

they are paired off against opponents at random. The winning boxer in each bout progresses to the next match until two boxers compete for gold and silver medals. The two losing semi-finalists both receive bronze medals. Today, an Olympic medal is considered a springboard for a young boxer to start a professional career. Muhammad Ali, Sugar Ray Leonard, Wladimir Klitschko and Amir Khan are just some of the boxers who took this route.

Computer Scoring

At major amateur competitions, the five ringside judges have two scoring buttons, one for each boxer, linked to a computer. If a scoring punch is hit, the judge presses the button. If three of the five judges do this within a second of each other, the computer registers a point. If one boxer gets 20 points ahead of his opponent, the referee automatically stops the fight. Scoring can be controversial. At the 1988 Olympics, Roy Jones appeared to cruise to victory in the light middleweight final as he landed 86 punches to Park Si-Hun's 32, yet three of the judges awarded the fight to the South Korean. The three judges were later suspended.

Vasyl Lomachenko (right) of the Ukraine tussles with China's Li Yang on his way to winning their 2008 Olympic quarter-final.

TURNING PROFESSIONAL

While many boxers, even after winning major amateur titles, choose to stay amateur, others cannot resist turning professional in the hope of fame, fortune and major titles.

Match-making

A boxer's manager handles the business side of boxing, leaving the trainer to develop the boxer's fitness, skills and tactics. The manager also chooses early fights, often fewer than 12 rounds, against opponents picked to not be too much of a threat. Amir Khan's first four fights, for example, were over four rounds. Match-making in boxing is an art, with the manager looking for enticing fights but ones that his boxer will hope to win. Too cautious an approach can sometimes backfire. Audley Harrison turned professional after winning Olympic gold in 2000, but has been criticised during his professional career for avoiding dangerous opponents.

MAD FACT

In 1975, Saensak Muangsurin of Thailand fought for the WBC lightweight title in only his third professional fight and won.

Promoter and manager Frank Warren (right) sits ringside at a fight next to Don King, the most famous promoter in the world. Both these men wield much power when it comes to organising boxing bouts, representing fighters and promoting events.

Joe Calzaghe (right) and Bernard Hopkins both land punches in their 2008 bout which was marketed as the 'Battle of the Planet' by the promoters. Calzaghe won the fight.

A Boxer's Purse

The manager negotiates with a fight promoter (see p39) about how much the boxer receives for taking on the fight. This sum is known as the boxer's purse. These negotiations can be long and hard as both manager and promoter seek to make as much money as possible. At the lower end of professional boxing, a purse may barely cover a boxer's expenses, but at the top end the sums can be enormous. For their 2008 fight, Joe Calzaghe and Bernard Hopkins both received a purse of US$3 million. In many situations, the holder of a major title can be assured more money than the challenger, unless the challenger is a massive box office draw and the champion holds a lesser title. For their 2007 superfight, Oscar de la Hoya was guaranteed US$23.3 million and Floyd Mayweather Jr US$10 million.

Taking the Knocks

The money a boxer can earn is not only based on his success and record in the ring but also his reputation and box office appeal. A boxer with an aggressive style who knocks out many of his opponents tends to be valued more by promoters than a more defensive boxer. Winning many bouts in a row is not always enough; these have to be against tough opponents and won in an exciting and convincing style.

MAD FACT

Vitali Klitschko currently holds the WBC heavyweight world title while his brother, Wladimir, holds the IBF and WBA. The two brothers have vowed that they will never fight one another.

TITLE FIGHTS

Many boxers start out by fighting for a national title and may go on to a continental title such as European champion before getting a chance to fight for a world title.

The Alphabet Men

A large number of organisations, nicknamed the alphabet men, offer their own championship titles for fighters to contend. The four major organisations are now considered to be the World Boxing Association (WBA), the World Boxing Council (WBC), the World Boxing Organisation (WBO) and the International Boxing Federation (IBF). In women's boxing, the situation is similar with a number of organisations, including the Women's International Boxing Federation (WIBF) and the International Female Boxers Association (WIBA).

US boxer Roy Jones Jr (left) and Puerto Rico's Felix Trinidad fight in New York in 2008. Both boxers were past their peak at the time, but the bout made around US$25 million in Pay Per View revenue alone.

David Haye celebrates his win over Enzo Maccarinelli in 2008 (see page 26). He is wearing the WBO, WBA, WBC and The Ring's world cruiserweight championship belts.

Boxing Politics

In men's boxing, holding a number of world titles at a certain weight division makes a boxer a unified or undisputed champion. However, in practice, things get more complicated. Boxing organisations create new, interim or temporary titles, whilst boxers can be stripped of a title if they refuse to fight an opponent picked by an organisation as their official challenger or if the negotiations about their next fight break down. Boxers cannot hold world titles in different weight divisions, so to fight a prized opponent in a different division they may choose to give up or vacate a title. For example, David Haye vacated his cruiserweight titles so that he could box as a heavyweight.

Fight Finance

The on-off nature of eagerly anticipated bouts can frustrate fight fans. When a major bout is agreed, promoters do all they can to ensure that publicity and marketing drives generate as much interest and money as possible. Money is made from the sales of tickets for the bout and, for bigger fights, the sales of merchandise and, particularly, rights for television companies to broadcast the bout. The rise of Pay Per View, where individuals subscribe and pay a fee to watch a single boxing match, has boosted the money in major fights dramatically. The 2007 de la Hoya versus Mayweather fight generated ticket sales of US$19 million – a record in itself. But more than 2.2 million people bought Pay Per View options to watch the fight worth an estimated US$120 million.

STAT ATTACK

Recent Pay Per View Top Earners

Oscar de la Hoya: US$612 million

Mike Tyson: US$545 million

Evander Holyfield: US$543 million

SUPER FIGHTS

With so many different organisations and a large number of weight divisions, it can be hard to judge who really are the best boxers. Ring ratings and expert opinion can be used as a guide, but it is the coming together of two very highly ranked boxers in a superfight that is a true test of ability.

Pound-for-Pound

A number of magazines, television broadcasters and other organisations offer 'pound-for-pound' ratings. These take boxers' differing weights out of the equation and instead focusing on their style, resilience, punching power and recent results. Any such list is purely opinion and generates much debate and discussion. *The Ring* magazine is often considered the most authoritative source of pound-for-pound ratings.

Juan Manuel Marquez (left) battles with the previously unbeaten Cuban boxer Joel Casamayor in their 2008 superfight. The fight ended when Marquez knocked out Casamayor in the 11th round.

Superfights Today

Today, with the masses of hype and publicity in boxing, almost any bout for a world championship is labelled as a superfight. Many genuine superfights still occur, especially when two champion boxers come to the ring both with unblemished records. In 2007 for example, Ricky Hatton, unbeaten in 43 fights, faced Floyd Mayweather Jr (unbeaten in 38 bouts) in Las Vegas in a superfight that Mayweather won. Other superfights have seen rematches as the beaten boxer seeks revenge, leading to a series of close fights between two boxers like the three bouts between Americans, Mickey Ward and Arturo Gatti in 2002-2003.

Hector 'Macho' Camacho enters the ring as a Roman gladiator. Grand entrances are a part of many superfights.

Epic Showdowns

There have been many epic fights between great boxers throughout boxing history. During the 1960s and 1970s, most attention was on the heavyweight division with Muhammad Ali, Joe Frazier, Ken Norton and George Foreman fighting each other. The 1975 Ali versus Joe Frazier bout in the Philippines, known as the 'Thrilla in Manilla', is regarded as one of the best heavyweight bouts of all time. During the 1980s and 1990s, many of the biggest fights in boxing moved away from the heavyweight division to the middle and welterweight divisions. In the 1980s, legendary fighters including Sugar Ray Leonard, Marvin Hagler, Thomas Hearns and Roberto Duran wowed audiences, while in the 1990s boxing fans eagerly anticipated bouts involving Roy Jones Jr, Oscar de la Hoya and Bernard Hopkins.

BOXING LEGENDS

The sport of boxing has seen some remarkable champions in its long history. Here are just five of the greatest boxing legends.

MAD FACT

George Foreman is the father of five sons, all of whom he named George!

Teofilo Stevenson

Born in 1952 in Cuba, Teofilo Stevenson stayed amateur all his career, despite offers to turn professional. His powerful punching style would have undoubtedly made him a professional boxing star but he contented himself by becoming the first boxer to win three Olympic gold medals in one weight class in 1972, 1976 and 1980. Stevenson also won three World Championship amateur titles in 1974 and 1978 and as a super-heavyweight in 1986.

Thomas Hearns

Thomas 'The Hit Man' Hearns had a distinguished amateur career with 155 victories before turning professional. He fought as a welterweight but in an era with some truly great fighters a little heavier than him around, from Iran Barkley to Marvin Hagler, Hearns moved up the weights to take them on. Possessing devastating boxing ability, in 1988 Hearns became the first boxer to win six world titles in different weight divisions.

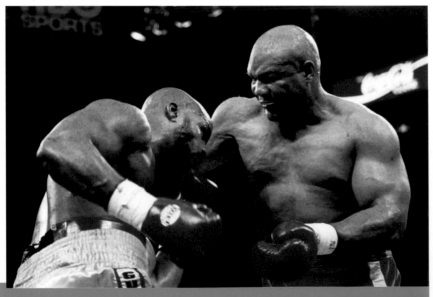

George Foreman (right) lands a short right punch during his record-breaking fight with Michael Moorer. Foreman wore the same red shorts he had worn in his fight with Muhammad Ali 20 years earlier.

George Foreman

Foreman was a formidable heavyweight boxer, winning the Olympic gold medal in 1968. He knocked out Joe Frazier to win the world title in 1973 and went on to win 24 fights in a row, all with knock outs, until his epic defeat to Muhammad Ali in 1974. Foreman retired in 1977, but returned to boxing a decade later and, in 1994 at the age of 45, knocked out Michael Moorer to become boxing's oldest heavyweight champion.

Marvin Hagler

One of the most fearsome middleweights ever in boxing, 'Marvellous' Marvin Hagler won 57 amateur fights before turning professional. After several defeats in 1976 to unremarkable middleweights, Hagler stepped up a gear and was not beaten again for 10 years. He destroyed British boxer Alan Minter to win a world title and, in 1985, he and Thomas Hearns fought one of the most brutal bouts in boxing history. Both landed dozens of punches before Hagler knocked Hearns out in the third round. Losing by a split-decision to Sugar Ray Leonard in 1987, Hagler retired from boxing.

MAD //// //// FACT

Marvin Hagler was a powerful puncher. Of his 62 winning professional fights, only 10 were not won by a knockout.

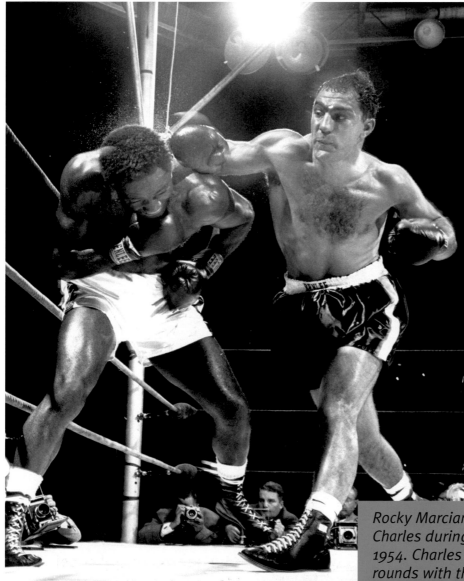

Rocky Marciano (right) punches Ezzard Charles during their epic bout in September 1954. Charles was the only boxer to last 15 rounds with the formidable Marciano.

Rocky Marciano

The Brockton Blockbuster as he was nicknamed, began boxing in the US army during World War II and exploded onto the heavyweight scene after the war. He was knocked down in the first round of his world championship fight against Jersey Joe Walcott in 1952, but stormed back to knock out the champion in the 13th round. He defended his world title six times and retired in 1956 with a record of 49 fights and 49 wins, the only heavyweight world champion to retire undefeated.

GLOSSARY

Bare-knuckle boxing   Fights, mostly held in the past, between boxers without protective gloves on their hands.

Belt   An imaginary line from a boxer's navel to the top of the hips, below which opposing boxers are not allowed to hit.

Bob   To bounce on the balls of the feet.

Bout   A boxing contest. Also known as a fight or match.

Break   A referee's order for boxers to separate if they are in a clinch.

Clinch   The act of one or both boxers holding the other in a way that stops punches being made.

Corner   The junction of the ropes where a boxer rests between rounds.

Count   Counting for up to ten seconds by the referee, after which, if a boxer

is still down, the referee declares a loss by knockout.

Counterattack   To throw punches and attack just as or after the opponent attacks.

Cuts-man   A person in a boxer's corner who treats cuts and swellings to the face of a boxer during a fight.

Knockout   A ruling by which the referee stops the bout and declares a boxer the winner if the opponent has been down for the count of ten.

MRI scan   Short for magnetic resonance imaging, this is a type of medical scan that is often used to assess the condition of parts of the brain.

Orthodox   A boxing stance in which the left foot is placed ahead of the right.

Outclassed   A ruling by which the referee stops the bout because a boxer is taking excessive punishment, and declares the opponent the winner.

Power punches   Solid punches to the chin, head or body that inflict damage to an opponent.

Professional   Paid to box.

Reach   The distance a boxer's punch can travel. Reach is measured either from fingertip to fingertip of both arms outstretched or from the armpit to fingertips of one arm.

Round One of a series of periods of time, separated by rests, that make up a boxing bout.

Southpaw Usually, the stance of a left-handed boxer who stands the opposite way round to a boxer with an orthodox stance.

Sparring A form of training in which a boxer fights against a partner in the ring while wearing a helmet and other protective guards and clothing.

Split decision A result which occurs when two of the three judges score one boxer as the winner, and the remaining judge scores the other boxer as the victor.

Superfight The nickname given to a major bout, which is usually a world championship fight between two very highly-rated boxers.

Unanimous decision When all of the judges scoring a bout award the fight to one boxer.

Weave To make turning and twisting movements to avoid being hit by an opponent's punches.

Weigh-in A pre-fight occasion during which boxers are weighed to make sure they are within the limits of their weight division for the fight.

WEBSITES

HTTP://NEWS.BBC.CO.UK/SPORTI/HI/BOXING/4721089.STM

This BBC boxing page gives details of the original eight weight divisions in boxing along with some of each division's greatest fighters.

WWW.SECONDSOUT.COM

A boxing magazine on the web with news, interviews and profiles of leading boxers.

WWW.AIBA.ORG

The official website of the International Boxing Association (AIBA) includes an events calendar, news and results.

WWW.BOXREC.COM/MEDIA/INDEX.PHP/MAIN_PAGE

A boxing encyclopedia on the web, with information about boxers and the rules of the sport, a gallery of images and a glossary of boxing terms.

WWW.FRANKWARREN.TV/V6/INDEX.PHP

The website of promoter and manager Frank Warren includes images of boxers at press conferences, in training and at the weigh in.

WWW.SADDOBOXING.COM/BOXINGLINKS/INDEX.PHP

A great collection of links to other boxing web pages, including boxers' official websites.

Note to parents and teachers:

Every effort has been made by the publishers to ensure that these websites are suitable for children, that they are of the highest educational value, and that they contain no inappropriate or offensive material. However, because of the nature of the Internet, it is impossible to guarantee that the contents of these sites will not be altered. We strongly advise that Internet access is supervised by a responsible adult.

INDEX